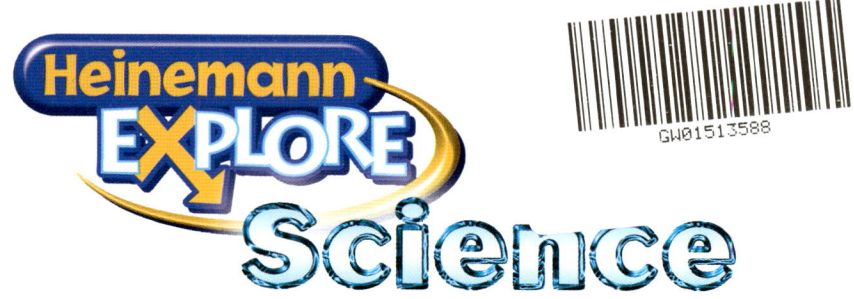

Student Book
New International Edition

Grade 2

Tara Lievesley, Deborah Herridge
Series editor: John Stringer

PEARSON

Pearson Education Limited is a company incorporated in England and Wales having its registered office at Edinburgh Gate, Harlow, Essex, CM20 2JE.

Registered company number: 872828

www.pearsonglobalschools.com

Text © Pearson Education Limited 2012
First published 2003. This edition published 2012.

16 15 14 13 12
IMP 10 9 8 7 6 5 4 3 2 1

British Library Cataloguing in Publication Data
A catalogue record for this book is available from the British Library

ISBN 978 0 435 13356 6

Copyright notice
All rights reserved. No part of this publication may be reproduced in any form or by any means (including photocopying or storing it in any medium by electronic means and whether or not transiently or incidentally to some other use of this publication) without the written permission of the copyright owner, except in accordance with the provisions of the Copyright, Designs and Patents Act 1988 or under the terms of a licence issued by the Copyright Licensing Agency, Saffron House, 6–10 Kirby Street, London EC1N 8TS (www.cla.co.uk). Applications for the copyright owner's written permission should be addressed to the publisher.

Edited by Janice Curry
Designed by Scout Design Associates
Original illustrations © Pearson Education Limited, 2003, 2009, 2012
Illustrated by Simon Rumble, Beehive Illustration Limited
Cover photo/illustration © Charles McClean, Alamy Images
Indexed by Indexing Specialists (UK) Ltd
Printed in Malaysia, CTP-KHL

Acknowledgements

The author and publisher would like to thank the following individuals and organisations for permission to reproduce photographs:

(Key: b-bottom; c-centre; l-left; r-right; t-top)

Alamy Images: 2b, 6cl, 6bl, 14 (granite), 14 (Rock salt), 14bl, 15bl, 29 (Bike Light), 29 (bike reflector), 29 (safe jacket), 31r, 33br, 35cr, 42bl, 47tr, 52cr, 52bl, 52br, 53br, 59cr, 64cr; **Corbis:** 1cr, 10tr, 62cr; **Fotolia.com:** 8t, 8l, 8r, 9t, 9b, 11tr, 11cl, 14 (Red granite), 17tr, 19 (sleeping bag), 19 (tooth brushes), 19cl, 19bl, 19br, 25br, 32bl, 32br, 38cr, 42 (Computer), 42 (kitchen), 42 (phone), 42 (TV), Marsy 21r; **Getty Images:** 3tr, 10bl, 63tr, 63bl; **Glow Images:** 1tl, 2cr, 3bl, 5br, 10br, 15tr, 39br, 47cr; **Reuters:** 65br; **Science Photo Library Ltd:** 44cr, 45t, 45b; **Shutterstock.com:** 6 (Butterfly), 6 (date tree), 6 (fish), 6 (Hibiscus Flower), 6 (Tiger), 21 (butter), 21 (can), 21 (egg), 21 (ice), 21 (log), 21 (rubber band), 28 (candle), 28 (Lamp), 28 (stars), 28 (street light), 28 (Sun), 29 (Diamond), 29 (mirror), 43tr, 43c, 43cl, 49bl, 52c, 53cl, 55b, 61cl

All other images © Pearson Education

Every effort has been made to contact copyright holders of material reproduced in this book. Any omissions will be rectified in subsequent printings if notice is given to the publishers. In some instances we have been unable to trace the owners of copyright material, and we would appreciate any information that would enable us to do so.

Contents

How to use this book	iv
Unit 1: Living things in the environment	**1**
Let's explore!	2
Home sweet home	4
Grouping animals	6
Caring for our environment	8
The weather	10
Unit 1: Review	12
Unit 2: Materials	**13**
What are rocks?	14
Hard as nails?	16
Natural or not?	18
All change!	20
Heating up	22
Disappearing acts	24
Unit 2: Review	26
Unit 3: Light and dark	**27**
Source of light	28
Our Sun	30
Using light	32
Shady shadows	34
Exploring shadows	36
Changing shadows	38
Unit 3: Review	40

Unit 4: Electricity	**41**
Bright sparks	42
What is a circuit?	44
What? No electricity?	46
Making models	48
Circuit pictures	50
Attention seekers	52
Unit 4: Review	54
Unit 5: Earth and beyond	**55**
A galaxy far away	56
Spinning around	58
Moving shadows	60
Happy Birthday Earth!	62
Night and day	64
Unit 5: Review	66
Unit Checklists	**67**
Unit 1: Living things in the environment	67
Unit 2: Materials	68
Unit 3: Light and dark	69
Unit 4: Electricity	70
Unit 5: Earth and beyond	71
Glossary	72
Index	74

How to use this book

At the beginning of each Unit there are lists of things you should already know or be able to do.

This shows words in the Unit that are important. Learn and use them.

This box tells you what the lesson is about.

Think about these questions. By the end of the Unit you will know how to answer them.

Try these activities. Your teacher will help you.

Find out what coloured words in bold mean in the Glossary at the back of the book.

These boxes give you some fascinating facts.

This box tells you what you will find out during the lesson. Your teacher will help you.

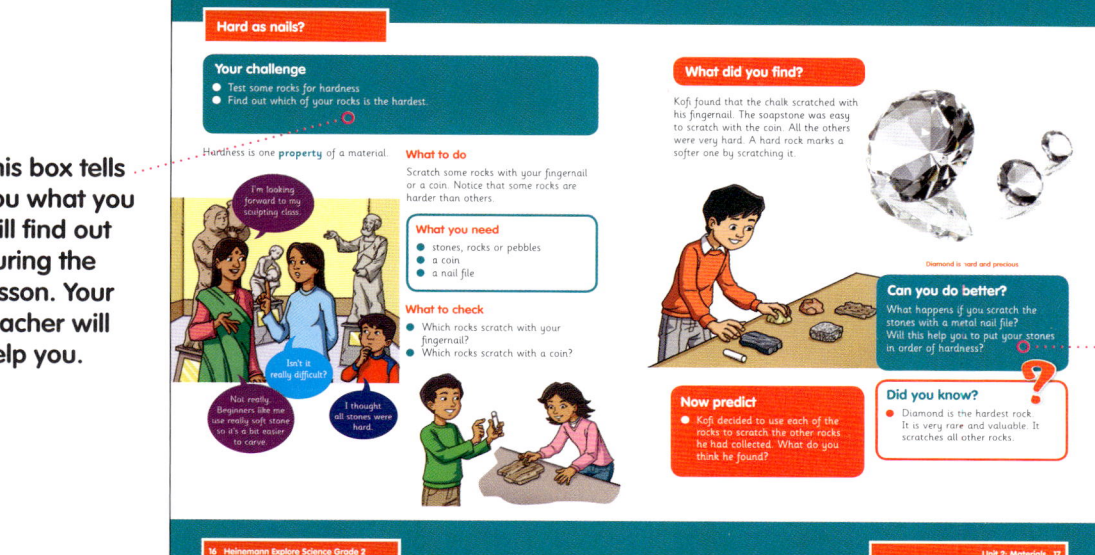

Use what you have learned to answer these questions.

Here you find answers to important questions.

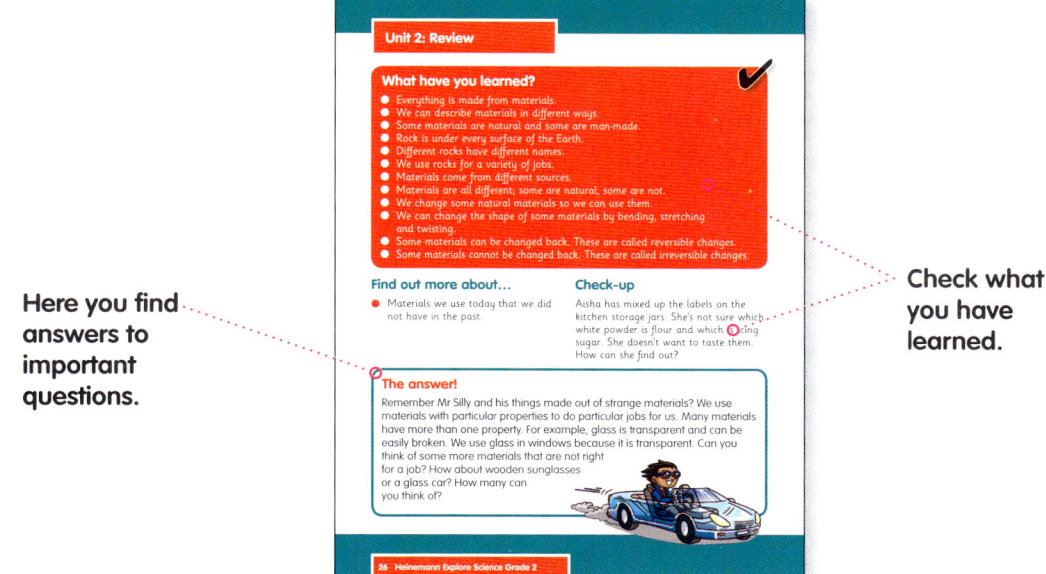

Check what you have learned.

How to use this book v

Unit 1: Living things in the environment

Polar bear

How many living things can you see around your school? Are there any polar bears? Are there any penguins? What about a big cactus or a tall redwood tree? Would these animals and plants survive where you live?

What do you know?
- Plants and animals are living things
- Different plants and animals are found in different places in the world
- The weather can be different in different places and at different times of the year.

Skills check
Can you...
- ask questions and try to answer them?
- make careful observations?
- find and compare things that are the same and things that are different?

A hot, wet tropical environment

Words to learn
environment
extinct
grow
habitat
hibernate
hibernation
migrate
migration
minibeast
organism
weather

Let's find out...
Nature reserves are parts of the **environment**. They are places where animals and plants are looked after. No one can build on the land or change anything in these places. Why do we have nature reserves?

Let's explore!

Things to learn
- There are different animals and plants in your local environment
- Not all parts of the environment are the same
- Some animals and plants are only found in some places.

What is the environment?

The environment is everywhere plants and animals live. It is where they can **grow** and produce new plants or animals. What is your environment like where you live? A plant or animal's environment is also affected by the **weather** where it lives.

The weather in this seashore environment is hot

The weather in this mountain environment can be very cold

Things to do

Sharing an environment

Think about where you live. Do you share your environment with other animals? Are they all welcome?

In the place where you live, record the animals and plants you can find.

Dig deeper

Find out:
- how many different living things are around school
- how they live in this environment
- what dangers they face
- show what you have found to your classmates.

This tiny frog lives in a jungle environment

I wonder...

What is the strangest place to find life?

Cockroaches live in many different conditions

Make sure you wash your hands after handling plants, animals or soil.

Did you know?

- Scientists are discovering new plants and new animals all of the time. A frog the size of a pea has just been found in Borneo for the first time.

Unit 1: Living things in the environment 3

Home sweet home

Things to learn
- A habitat is the home of a plant or animal
- Different plants and animals live in different habitats.

Where I live

A **habitat** is the home of a plant or animal.

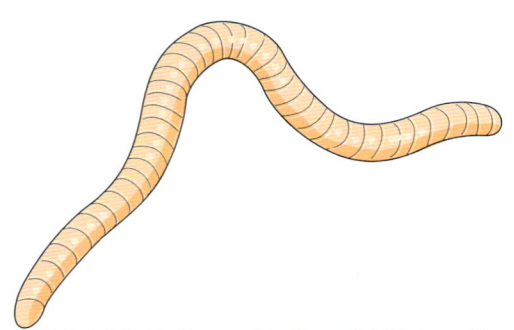

My habitat is the cool, dark earth. What am I?

My habitat is the hot, dry desert. What am I?

I live in flooded fields. What am I?

I live in the sea. I couldn't survive in the desert or in the earth. What am I?

Things to do

The wrong place

Something's wrong here. These plants and animals are in the wrong habitats.

What's wrong in this picture?

I wonder...
Is there any animal that can live in any habitat?

Dig deeper

Find out:
- how some animals move to a new habitat when the seasons change. We call this movement from one place to another **migration**.

Did you know?

- Some animals slow down in the colder winter months. They sleep for most of the time. We call this **hibernation**. Many animals **hibernate** to survive the winter months.

Brown bears hibernate in winter

Grouping animals

Things to learn
- We call all living things organisms
- There are similarities and differences between plants and animals
- Living things can be grouped in different ways
- Humans belong to the animal group.

Same and different

Is this a plant or an animal? Sometimes it can be difficult to tell.

Is a sea anemone a plant or animal?

We call all living things **organisms**. We can group them in different ways.

Which are plants?
Which are animals?

Is this an insect or a flower?

Are humans animals?

What do we share with other animals?

6 Heinemann Explore Science Grade 2

Things to do

Animals

Look at these animals. Have you seen any around your school? Are there more in some places than in others?

Class 2 hunted for animals around their school. This is what they found.

- Make a chart of the animals you find.
- Where did you find the most?
- Present your chart to your classmates.

Dig deeper

Find out:
- how we group animals. Birds are one group. Fish are another. What other groups do you know?

I wonder...

Scorpions and spiders are very different. How are they different?

Did you know?

- We may call tiny animals **minibeasts**.
- Minibeasts are not born looking like their parents. They change as they grow from egg to adult.

Unit 1: Living things in the environment   7

Caring for our environment

Things to learn
- Animals live in habitats that are special to them
- Living things and their habitats need protecting
- Humans can damage the environment.

Dead as a Dodo

Have you ever seen a Dodo? A Dodo was a bird with a big beak.

Dodos are **extinct**. There are none left alive in the world. People killed all the Dodos.

An Amur leopard

A scarlet macaw

A Dodo

Animals in danger

Other animals are in danger too. The Amur leopard is close to extinction. The scarlet macaw is in danger because its habitat is being destroyed.

Things to do

In my backyard

Plants and animals where you live are in danger too. We must protect their habitats. Otherwise they may become extinct.

Even a road through a desert destroys habitats

Destroying forests destroys habitats. Plants and animals may become extinct.

People are destroying the rainforest

I wonder...

What can I do to protect plants and animals? Make it a habit to care for habitats.

Dig deeper

Find out:
- about the Worldwide Fund for Nature. What do groups like this do?

Did you know?

- Some scientists study the environment. We call this ecology.

The weather

Things to learn
- Different countries have different weather
- Scientists observe and measure the weather
- By looking for patterns we can predict the weather.

Whatever the weather

What is the weather like today?

Weather is the mixture of sunshine, rain and wind. All weather is three things: heat from the Sun, moving air and water.

Strong winds can cause damage!

Extreme weather

Sometimes the weather can cause damage! Hurricanes and tornadoes are very strong winds. They can pull up trees and flatten houses.

A drought is a long time without rain. Rivers dry up and plants die because they have no water.

We wear different clothes in different weather

The ground can crack in a drought

Things to do

Tomorrow's weather

Meteorologists are scientists who study the weather. They measure the weather. Over many years they can see patterns in the weather. They can use these to predict how it will be in the future.

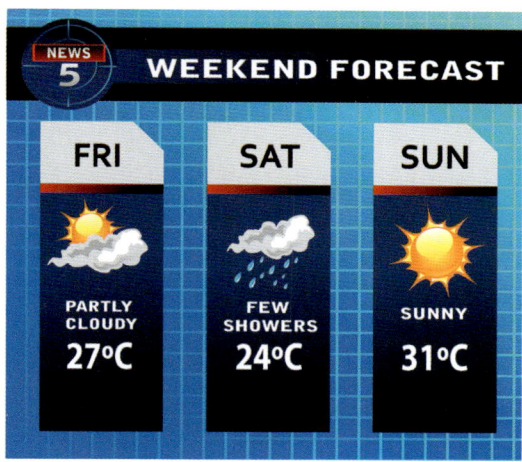

A weather forecast

How can you collect information about the weather where you live?

I wonder...
Do plants change with changing weather?

Measuring the winds

We talk about winds coming from directions of the compass. The ancient Greeks had special names for the winds: Boreas, for the wind from the North, Auster from the South, Eurus from the East and Zephyr from the West.

Strong winds help these surfers move fast

Today we have special names for special winds like the Shamal in the Arabian Gulf or the Aejej in Morocco.

Think about how you could measure and compare different winds.

Dig deeper
Find out:
- more about how weather is forecast.

Did you know?
- The sunniest place in the world is Yuma in Arizona, USA. The Sun shines for almost 12 hours each **day**.

Unit 1: Living things in the environment 11

Unit 1: Review

What have you learned?
- Plants and animals are living things. They are all organisms.
- You can name some different animals and plants in your local environment.
- A habitat is a place where plants and animals live naturally.
- Different plants and animals live in different habitats.
- There are similarities and differences between plants (and animals).
- You can group living things in different ways.
- Humans belong to the animal group.
- Humans can damage the environment and we should care for it.
- Different places in the world have different weather.
- By studying patterns in the weather we can predict what it will be like in the future.

Find out more about...
- extreme weather
- what does it do?

Check-up
Rani noticed a lot of rubbish being left in the river near to school. She worried about the safety of the river animals. Why should she be concerned?

The answer!
Remember the question about why we have nature reserves?
Now you know that some animals and plants are in danger of losing their homes or their habitat. Sometimes this is because of things that people do. We make nature reserves to protect special habitats and the animals and plants in them. They are protected from extinction.

Unit 2: Materials

How many materials can you see around your school? How are the materials used?

What do you know?

- Everything is made from materials
- We can describe materials in different ways
- Some materials are natural and some are man-made.

Words to learn

artificial, bend, change, compare, cool, dissolve, heat, material, melt, processed, property, reversible, solid, stretch, **substance**, twist

Skills check

Can you...
- ask questions and try to answer them?
- make careful observations?
- predict what will happen in an investigation?

How many different materials you can see?

Let's find out...

Mr Silly is always mixing things up. His bed is made of jelly, his bicycle is made of paper and his shoes are made of concrete.

Why are these not the right materials?

What are rocks?

Things to learn
- Rock is under the whole surface of the Earth
- Different rocks have different names
- We use rocks for a variety of jobs.

Under our feet

Look down at your feet. If you dig down you will find rock.

Our planet is made from rock. There is rock under every surface of the Earth; under the desert, and under the sea.

There are different types of rocks. They all look different from each other. Some are useful to us in different ways.

Different types of rock

Some rocks were laid down in layers like these

Ancient rocks

Some rocks were made when the hot Earth first **cooled** down millions of years ago. Some were squashed. Some were **melted**. Some were made at the bottom of the sea.

Things to do

Types of rocks

Some rocks burst out of the Earth when volcanoes erupt. The hot lava hardens into new rock.

What's inside?

Some rocks contain the remains of plants and animals. They have been turned into stone. We call them fossils.

Liquid lava from a volcano cools to make volcanic rock

Fossils are the remains of plants and animals turned to stone

Dig deeper

Find out:
- the different ways we use rocks.

Did you know?

- Sir Richard Owen, a British scientist, first gave the dinosaur its name. It means 'terrible lizard'.

I wonder...

Is your home made of rock?

Hard as nails?

Your challenge
- Test some rocks for hardness
- Find out which of your rocks is the hardest.

Hardness is one **property** of a material.

What to do
Scratch some rocks with your fingernail or a coin. Notice that some rocks are harder than others.

What you need
- stones, rocks or pebbles
- a coin
- a nail file

What to check
- Which rocks scratch with your fingernail?
- Which rocks scratch with a coin?

I'm looking forward to my sculpting class.

Isn't it really difficult?

Not really. Beginners like me use really soft stone so it's a bit easier to carve.

I thought all stones were hard.

What did you find?

Kofi found that the chalk scratched with his fingernail. The soapstone was easy to scratch with the coin. All the others were very hard. A hard rock marks a softer one by scratching it.

Diamond is hard and precious

Can you do better?

What happens if you scratch the stones with a metal nail file? Will this help you to put your stones in order of hardness?

Now predict

- Kofi decided to use each of the rocks to scratch the other rocks he had collected. What do you think he found?

Did you know?

- Diamond is the hardest rock. It is very rare and valuable. It scratches all other rocks.

Unit 2: Materials 17

Natural or not?

Things to learn
- Materials come from different sources
- Materials are all different; some are natural, some are not
- We change some natural materials so we can use them.

What am I?

"We dig it out of the ground so yes, it must be natural."

"Clay is a natural material isn't it?"

"But, when we **heat** it and turn it into pots, is it still natural?"

What do you think?

Things to do

Natural changes

Rocks are natural. So are wood and wool.

Natural wool comes from a sheep. We **change** it to use it. We spin it and knit it into jumpers. It is still a natural material but it is changed in some way or **processed**.

Look around the classroom. Can you see examples of natural materials that have been processed?

I made it myself

Some materials have been made by people. We call these materials **artificial**.

Think about the things you are wearing and the things you see around you at school.

Make a list of things that are made of natural materials. Make another list of things that are made of artificial materials.

Which is the longer list? Why do you think this is? Explain why to your classmates.

I wonder…
Are your clothes artificial or natural? How can you find out?

Dig deeper
Find out:
- about processed foods and artificial colourings.

Did you know?
- Nylon was the first artificial fibre. Nylon clothes are completely man-made.

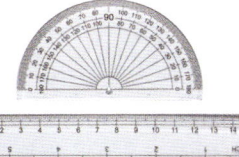
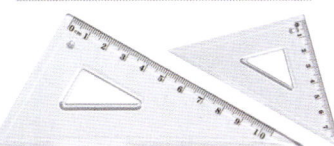

Artificial materials

All change!

Things to learn
- Some materials can be changed
- We can change the shape of some materials by bending, stretching and twisting
- Some things cannot be changed back.

Changing shape

I'm trying to make models for my farm but Rohan keeps squashing them!

I suppose the good thing about Plasticine is that you can keep changing its shape. I can make my animals again.

It's time for his bath now so you'll be left in peace.

Reversible or not?

When some things change shape we can easily change them back — like clay or Plasticine. We call this a **reversible** change. It can go back to the way it was.

Things to do

Will it change?

Look at these materials.

- Can we change them? How?
- Which can be **bent**?
- Which can be **stretched**?
- Which can be **twisted**?
- Is the change reversible or not?

I wonder…

What materials stretch? What materials can you twist?

Dig deeper

Find out:
- how metal can be changed
- what an alloy is.

Did you know?

- Your bathroom is mostly made from rock.
- Basins and toilets are made from baked clay.
- Tiles are made from baked clay.
- Pipes and taps are made from metal – made from rocks.

Unit 2: Materials

Heating up

Things to learn
- Some materials change when they are heated
- Some of these changes are reversible
- Some of these changes are **irreversible**.

Melting moments

Many food materials are changed by heat. Some become **liquid**, or melt.

What could stop chocolate from melting on a warm day?

What other foods melt in the Sun?

Things to do

Marvellous mixtures

Anya is making cakes

Dig deeper

Find out:
- how ice cream is made
- if the change is reversible when ice cream melts.

Did you know?
- Chocolate grows on trees! It is made from Cacao beans.

What can Anya do to change this **solid** chocolate, marshmallows and breakfast cereal into cakes for the party?

I wonder…
Does chocolate change when it is melted? Is the change reversible?

South Americans discovered chocolate, centuries ago

Disappearing acts

Your challenge
- Find out which materials dissolve and which do not.

Amina didn't eat the sweet. It was made of sugar and it **dissolved** in her mouth.

What to do
Try mixing some materials in water.

Make a recording sheet for your results.

Compare the results.

What you need
- salt, white sugar, flour, rice, brown sugar
- water

What to check
- What must you keep the same to make your test fair?

What did you find?

These are Amina and Khalifa's results:

Substance	Add cold water	What the water looked like
white sugar	dissolved after stirring	clear
brown sugar	dissolved after stirring	clear but brown coloured
flour	scattered through the water when we stirred it	cloudy with layer of powder on the bottom
salt	dissolved after stirring	clear
rice	on bottom of cup	water was clear but rice sank to bottom of cup

Now predict

How would the results change if they used warm water?

Did you know?

- The world's largest lollipop was made in 2009 by New Yorker Ashrita Furman. The lollipop weighed 3 041 kg (6 706 pounds).

Can you do better?

The children stirred the materials in the water — does that make a difference?

Unit 2: Review

What have you learned?

- Everything is made from materials.
- We can describe materials in different ways.
- Some materials are natural and some are man-made.
- Rock is under every surface of the Earth.
- Different rocks have different names.
- We use rocks for a variety of jobs.
- Materials come from different sources.
- Materials are all different; some are natural, some are not.
- We change some natural materials so we can use them.
- We can change the shape of some materials by bending, stretching and twisting.
- Some materials can be changed back. These are called reversible changes.
- Some materials cannot be changed back. These are called irreversible changes.

Find out more about…

- Materials we use today that we did not have in the past.

Check-up

Aisha has mixed up the labels on the kitchen storage jars. She's not sure which white powder is flour and which is icing sugar. She doesn't want to taste them. How can she find out?

The answer!

Remember Mr Silly and his things made out of strange materials? We use materials with particular properties to do particular jobs for us. Many materials have more than one property. For example, glass is transparent and can be easily broken. We use glass in windows because it is transparent. Can you think of some more materials that are not right for a job? How about wooden sunglasses or a glass car? How many can you think of?

Unit 3: Light and dark

Look around you. Is it daytime? Are there lights in the room? How can you see things in front of you?

Imagine it is the middle of the night. What would the room look like now? How is it different?

What do you know?

- We need **light** to see
- When there is no light it is **dark**.

Skills check

Can you...
- make suggestions of how to investigate an idea?
- make observations and comparisons?
- begin to explain your observations?

Words to learn

bend	night
bright	reflect
brighter	shiny
candle	source
dark	Sun
day	torch
light	

How can I look for him? It is so dark. I can't see anything.

Let's find out...

Aditi has lost her pet cat. It's dark outside. The cat is black. How can she find it?

Source of light

Things to learn
- Light comes from different sources
- Some light sources are **brighter** than others
- Shiny objects reflect light.

> You must never look straight at the Sun. It can hurt your eyes.

Seeing in the dark

Rohan's Mum wants lights in her garden. Then she can see when it is dark.

These shiny mirrors and glass balls will light up the path nicely.

I don't think that will work Mum. They are just reflectors. They are not lights.

Who do you think is right? Why?

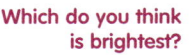

Which do you think is brightest?

What is a light source?

We say something is a light **source** when it has a light of its own. All of these are light sources. They make their own light.

28 Heinemann Explore Science Grade 2

Things to do

Shiny, shiny

Shiny objects don't make their own light. You cannot see them in the dark. A shiny object needs a light source to shine. They **reflect** light.

These shiny objects are not light sources. They reflect light back to us.

Shiny things reflect light

I wonder...

Why is there a light on the front of my bike and a reflector on the back?

Dig deeper

Find out:
- about celebrations using lights
- about the Hindu festival of Diwali and the British festival of 'bonfire night'.

Look at a can of pop. The bottom of the can is dull and curved. Can you see your face in it?

It reflects the light. But it does not make a good mirror!

Did you know?

- Some animals make their own light.

Unit 3: Light and dark 29

Our Sun

Things to learn
- The Sun is a source of light
- The Sun is our main source of light in the daytime
- Looking at the Sun can hurt our eyes.

People wearing sunglasses

The **Sun** is the Earth's main source of light. Never look straight at the Sun – even wearing sunglasses. It will hurt your eyes.

The Sun's light is bright in the daytime. The street lights are off

Why are the people wearing sunglasses in the daytime but not at **night**?

Some light is reflected from the Moon at night. The street lights are on

Things to do

Sunny days

This is too hot for me. I need to move into the shade where it is cooler.

The Sun gives us heat as well as light. The midday Sun shines straight down. It can burn your head, your shoulders and your feet. They face the Sun when you are standing.

I wonder…
Is there more than one Sun in the Universe?

Dig deeper
Find out:
- about animals that use the heat from the Sun to stay active.

A sunbathing lizard

Did you know?
- The surface of the Sun is extremely hot. It is about 5 500° Celsius.

Using light

Things to learn
- We need light to see
- Darkness is the absence of light
- We use light to see when it is dark.

Artificial light

We cannot see without a source of light. At night we use artificial light. Some lights guide us in the dark.

- Pilots use lights to land their planes at night.
- Ships use lighthouses to find their way in the dark.

Runway lights help pilots to land in the dark

This lighthouse guides ships near Istanbul

Things to do

The black box

Class 2 are investigating the dark. They made a black box from a shoe box. They painted the inside black. They cut a small hole in two sides.

They put different objects in the box. They cover up one hole, then look through the other.

- What will they see through the hole?
- What will they see when they uncover the second hole?

I wonder…

Where is it totally dark? What can you see?

Dig deeper

Find out:
- different ways we use lights to send messages.

Did you know?

- Some creatures living in the deep oceans make their own light. The lights help them to catch food.

An angler fish has a light on the end of a 'fishing rod'

Unit 3: Light and dark   33

Shady shadows

Things to learn
- Some materials block light
- Shadows are made when light is blocked.

Making a shadow

Some materials block light. The light cannot pass through them.

When this happens a shadow is made.

The plant's shadow matches its shape

The object blocks the light that strikes it.

The shape of the shadow matches the object that makes the shadow.

Abdul drew his shadow. He drew eyes on the shadow. He drew his belt on it. Why was he wrong?

What made these shadows?

Guess the object from the shape of the shadow.

Things to do

Make a shadow

You can make a shadow on a sunny day. Go outside. What shape can you make?

You block the light. The shadow is where the light does not go.

Indoor shadows

You can make shadows indoors too. What is blocking the light here?

I wonder...

Why can you never jump on your own shadow?

Indonesian shadow puppets block the light

Dig deeper

Find out:
- how shadow puppets can be used to tell a story.

Unit 3: Light and dark   35

Exploring shadows

Your challenge
- To find out which material makes the best shadow
- To plan an investigation.

Can you help the children find out which material makes the best shadow? How can they find out?

What to do
Put puppets made of different materials in front of a light to make shadows.

Make a table to record your results.

Discuss your results with your classmates.

What you need
- different materials like card, plastic, cloth and foil
- a bright light

What to check
- What must change?
- What can you observe?
- What must you keep the same to make it fair?

What did you find?
- Did all the materials make a shadow?
- What material made the darkest shadow?
- Were all the shadows sharp?
- Did some have a soft shadow around them?

Can you do better?
Can you sort your materials into one group that makes shadows and one group that does not?

Saad is curious about a clear plastic bottle. It is **transparent**.

I think if it is transparent, the material will not cast a shadow.

Now predict
Is Saad right? Try it.
What do you think will happen?
Were you surprised?

Unit 3: Light and dark 37

Changing shadows

Things to learn
- Light travels in straight lines
- When light is blocked a shadow is made
- You can change a shadow.

In straight lines

Light travels from the light source in straight lines. It cannot bend. When we make a shadow the light is blocked where the object is. The light around the object is not blocked.

Light travels in straight lines

These shadows are quite small. How can we make them bigger?

We could make the puppet shapes bigger. Would that work?

Making a change

Saad and Noor are practising their shadow puppet play.

How else can they make the shadows bigger?

What else can they move?

Things to do

Getting bigger

You can change a shadow by moving it closer to the source of light.

- Try it yourself. What do you discover?
- How can you make your shadow bigger?
- Who can make the biggest shadow?
- What happens when you move your light source?

I wonder…

Are shadows always black?

Why are some grey around the edges?

Dig deeper

Find out:
- about eclipses
- when the Earth throws a shadow
- when the Moon throws a shadow.

A solar eclipse: the Moon is between the Earth and the Sun

Unit 3: Light and dark 39

Unit 3: Review

What have you learned?
- We need light to see.
- When there is no light it is dark.
- Light comes from a source.
- Some light sources are brighter than others.
- Shiny objects reflect light.
- The Sun is our main source of light in the daytime.
- Looking at the Sun can hurt our eyes.
- We use light to see when it is dark.
- Some materials block light.
- We get shadows when light is blocked.
- You have found out which material makes the best shadow.
- Light travels in straight lines.
- You have found out that shadows can be changed.

Find out more about…
- changing shadows. How many ways can you find?

Check-up

Arundahti draws a picture of her shadow. Can you tell her where she has gone wrong?

The answer!

Remember the question about Aditi's lost cat? Finding something black on a dark night can be difficult. The night is never completely dark. There will always be some light from the stars. If we can see the Moon it will be reflecting light from the Sun. There is often light from streetlights or lights from houses. Aditi's cat has a collar made from a reflective material. It is very shiny. It is a good reflector of light. It will reflect light if a **torch** is shone on it. This will help Aditi find her pet.

Unit 4: Electricity

How many things use electricity? Some might use batteries. Some might use mains electricity. Some might use both! Electricity is really useful to us.

What do you know?

- Some things need electricity to work
- Batteries and mains are sources of electricity
- Mains electricity can be dangerous.

Skills check

Can you...
- ask questions and try to answer them?
- think about what might happen in an investigation?
- make careful observations?

Words to learn

appliance
battery
break
bulb
buzzer
circuit
compare
component
electricity
flow
mains electricity
switch
wire

Which electrical devices will work if there is a power cut?

Let's find out...

Electricity makes lots of things in our houses work.

If there were no electricity, what would not work in our homes?

Bright sparks

Things to learn
- Electricity can make things move, light up, heat up or produce sound
- Some appliances in our homes use mains electricity
- Some appliances in our homes use batteries
- Mains electricity can be dangerous.

How does it work?

Lots of things called **appliances** use electricity. Some are plugged in to the mains and some use **batteries**. **Mains** electricity is much stronger than battery electricity.

Which use batteries and which are plugged in?

Mains electricity can be dangerous!

Static electricity does not **flow**. But it can jump, as lightning!

42 Heinemann Explore Science Grade 2

Things to do

Around the house

Think about the rooms in your house. For each room draw or cut out catalogue pictures of things that use electricity. Which room has the most electrical appliances? Why?

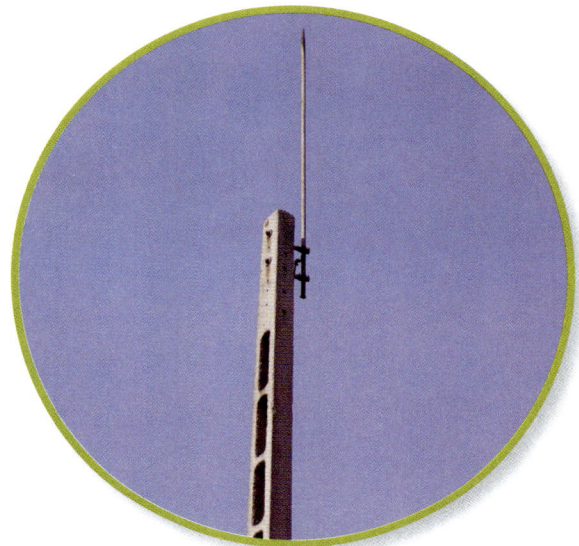

This metal rod is a lightning conductor

 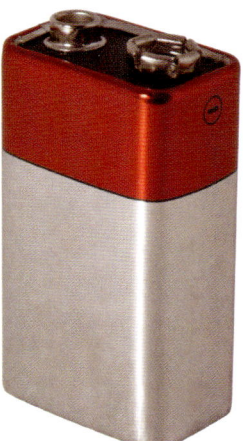

Batteries are different shapes and sizes

Dig deeper

Find out:
- how many different shapes and sizes of battery you can find
- the strength or voltage of each battery.

I wonder...

Why do tall buildings have metal rods from the top to the ground?

Did you know?

- Lightning is powerful and dangerous. It jumps from clouds to the Earth.

Unit 4: Electricity 43

What is a circuit?

Your challenge
- To make a simple circuit
- To find out what happens when we add bulbs to a circuit.

What to do

Try different ways of making a **circuit** to make a **bulb** light up.

Draw and label your different circuits.

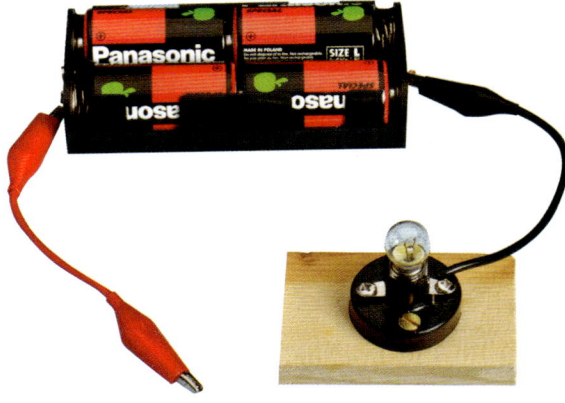

What you need
- a battery
- electric wires
- light bulb

What to check
- How many batteries, **wires** and lights will you need?
- Compare your circuit to your friend's. Are they the same?
- Add another bulb and more wires to your circuit. What do you think will happen?

What did you find?

- What do you notice about the two circuits the children made?
- What would a circuit with three bulbs in it look like?

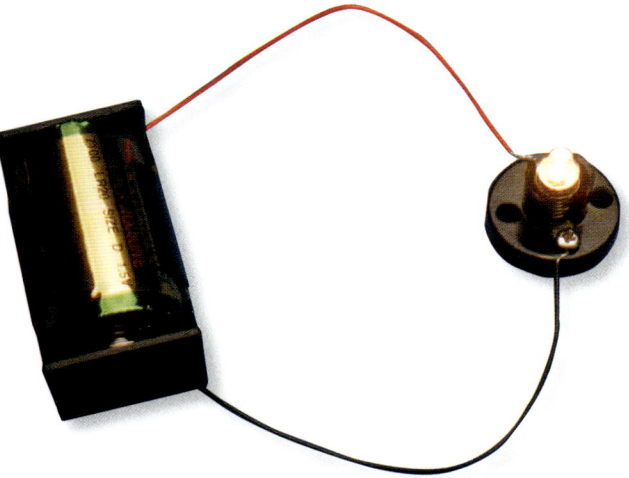

Can you do better?

- Did your circuits look like the children's?
- How bright are the bulbs? Do you notice a pattern? What is it?

Now predict

The children decided to add another battery to their circuit.

What do you think will happen? Why?

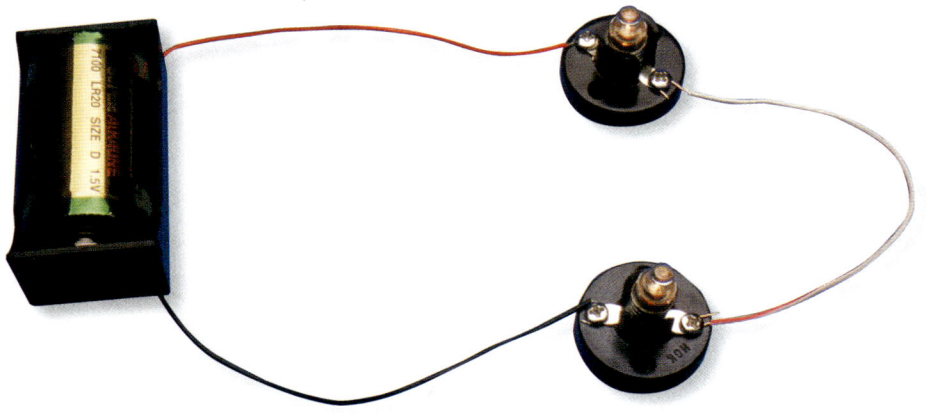

How are two bulbs different from one bulb? Why?

What? No electricity?

Things to learn
- Appliances use electricity to do different things
- Some appliances in our homes use mains electricity
- Electricity makes our lives easier.

What if?
Imagine a day without electricity. What would you miss the most?

Past times
Before people had electricity they had to light their homes in other ways. Find out how people in the past lit their homes.

What other sources of light are there?

Things to do

Your daily diary

Think of all the times in the day you use electricity. Keep a diary of the time and type of appliance you use. When do you use most electricity?

Saving electricity

Sometimes if we all use too much electricity at the same time there can be a power cut. There is no electricity. We need to use electricity sensibly and not waste it.

Dig deeper

Find out:
- which home appliances use the most electricity
- which use the least.

Thomas Edison and Joseph Swan both invented the electric light bulb. Sometimes two people can have the same idea!

I wonder...

How does electricity get to your home? Where is your electricity generated?

Did you know?

- Thomas Edison and Joseph Swan both invented the electric light bulb at about the same time.
- The difficult part was to find the right material for the filament - the wire that glows.

Unit 4: Electricity

Making models

Your challenge
- To make circuits using different components
- To make a model with a circuit in it.

The pieces of a circuit are called **components**. You can put components together in many different ways.

What to do

You can make models and light them up with battery electricity. You need a bulb in a circuit connected to the battery with wires.

Try using different types of components in your model.

Draw a plan of your model before you begin. Draw the circuit.

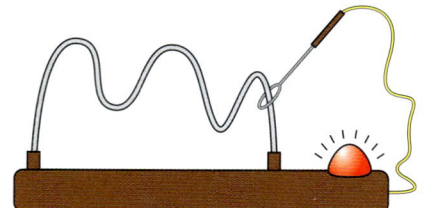

What you need
- battery
- wires
- **buzzer**
- motor
- bulbs

What to check
How do your components work? Can you use two different components in the same circuit? How?

Can you do better?
- How can you make the lights switch on and off in a model?
- What will you need to change in the circuit?
- How will you make your **switch**?

What did you find
Rohan's model car works well but the headlights are on all the time. How can he make it move without lights?

Now predict
Some switches stay on, like a light switch or TV. Others need to be held down, like a doorbell or a drill. What would be the best sort for your model?

Did you know?
- Buzzers are polarized. You must connect them the right way round in a circuit.

Unit 4: Electricity 49

Circuit pictures

Things to learn
- An electrical circuit must be complete to work
- We can draw circuits.

What's the problem?

Moser has made drawings of some circuits. Some are complete. Some are not.

He makes them but some do not work.

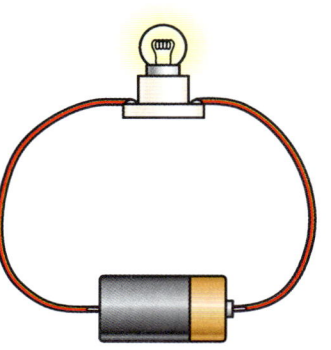
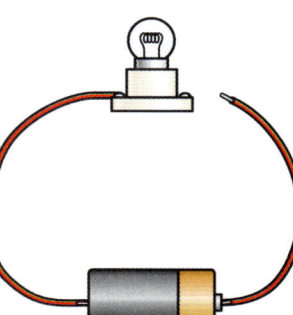
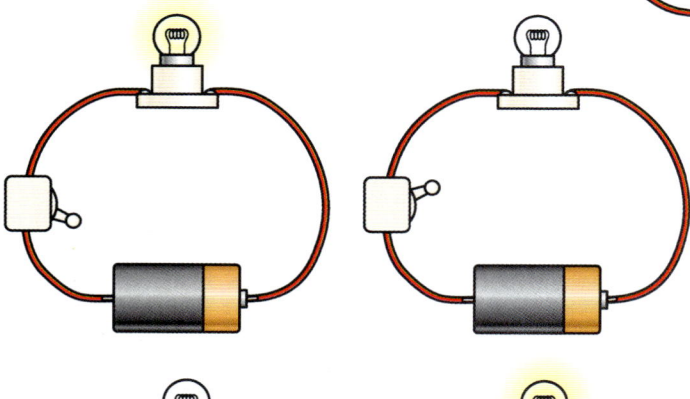
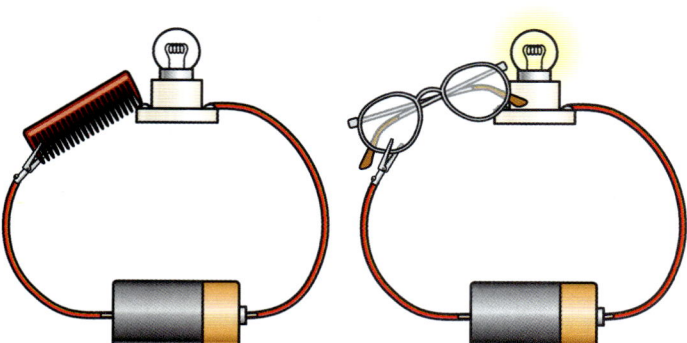

Unbroken

For a circuit to work, electricity must flow around the circuit without any **breaks**. The path of electricity is broken when there is a gap in the circuit. It is broken when part of the circuit is made of a material that electricity cannot pass through. Electricity cannot pass through plastic or wood.

Things to do

Apprentice electrician

Pretend that Moser is your trainee electrician. Make the circuits that he has made. Show him what he needs to do to fix them so that the bulbs light up.

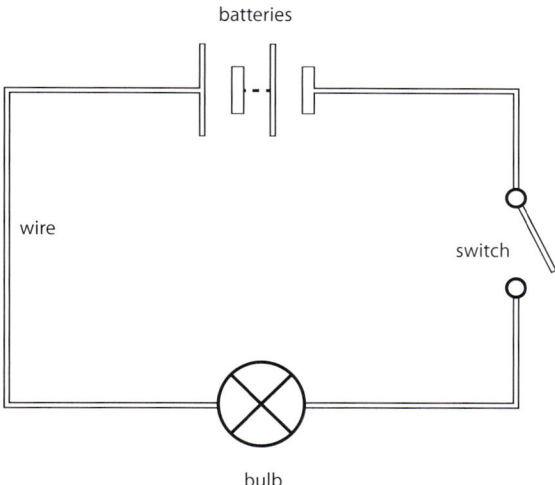

A circuit diagram

A circuit diagram

Sometimes electricians make pictures of circuits. The pictures record the circuits They help others copy the circuit.

- Choose one of your circuits. Make a diagram of it.
- Can your friend make the same circuit from your drawing?

I wonder...

Do all materials let electricity pass through?

Which materials let electricity pass through easily?

Dig deeper

Find out:
- about the symbols electricians use in their diagrams.

Did you know?

- Some modern lights are switched on just by touching the light with your hand.

Unit 4: Electricity 51

Attention seekers

Things to learn
- Electricity can be used to make movement, heat, light and sound
- We can use circuits for different purposes.

Look at me!

These all use electricity to attract attention using movement, light or sound.

- How do you think they work?
- What does the electricity do?

Things to do

Grab my attention

Design a device to get your teacher's attention. Make sure it uses an electric circuit. You can use lights or movement, sound or both!

- Draw a circuit diagram for your device before you make it.
- Can you spot any problems?
- Is it a complete circuit?
- Where will you put a switch?

Dig deeper

Find out:
- how electrical appliances help people with sight and hearing difficulties.

Wind power

Did you know?
- The electric eel is a fish that generates its own electricity.

An electric eel kills other fish with electricity

I wonder...
How can the wind generate electricity?

Unit 4: Electricity 53

Unit 4: Review

What have you learned?

- Electricity can make things move, light up, heat up and produce sound.
- Some appliances in our homes use mains electricity and some use electricity from batteries.
- Mains electricity can be dangerous.
- You can make a simple circuit.
- You know how electricity travels around a simple circuit.
- Circuits can contain different components.
- A switch can break the flow of electricity in a circuit.
- You can say why some circuits work and some do not.
- You can use symbols to draw a circuit.
- Electricity can be used to make our lives easier.

Find out more about...

- what an electrical conductor is
- why electrical wires are covered in plastic
- why we call plastic an insulator.

Check-up

Sunil's torch is not working. What should Sunil check to find out why his torch isn't working?

The answer!

Remember the question about what would not work in our homes if there was no electricity?

Now you know that we use two sorts of electricity: mains electricity and battery electricity. Large appliances use mains electricity – washing machines and fridges. We plug these machines into sockets. Smaller appliances, like torches and radios, use electricity from batteries.

Unit 5: Earth and beyond

The Universe is very big. No one knows how big it is. The Universe is made of huge masses of stars called **galaxies**. Our Sun, the **Earth** where we live and our **Moon** are part of one small galaxy called the **Milky Way**.

What do you know?

- The Earth is a **planet**
- The Sun is our nearest **star**
- The Earth and Sun are part of the **Universe**.

Skills check

Can you...
- suggest how to investigate an idea?
- make observations and comparisons?
- begin to explain your observations?

Words to learn

asteroid
axis
comet
Earth
galaxy
gnomon
Milky Way
Moon
orbit
planet
spin
star
Sun
sundial
Universe

Let's find out...

Anjuli lives in Delhi in India. She wants to call her Aunt to say Happy Birthday to her. Anjuli's Aunt lives in Los Angeles in America. Anjuli's Dad says she can't call just now because her Aunt will still be in bed!

Why is it night in some parts of the Earth when it is day in others?

Our Milky Way galaxy

A galaxy far away

Things to learn
- The Earth is a planet
- The Earth is one of eight known planets in the solar system
- The Sun is a star at the centre of the solar system.

Our solar family

Our Sun is a huge star made of burning gases. It gives us heat and light. Our Earth is part of a group of planets, moons, **comets** and **asteroids** spinning around our Sun. We call this family the solar system.

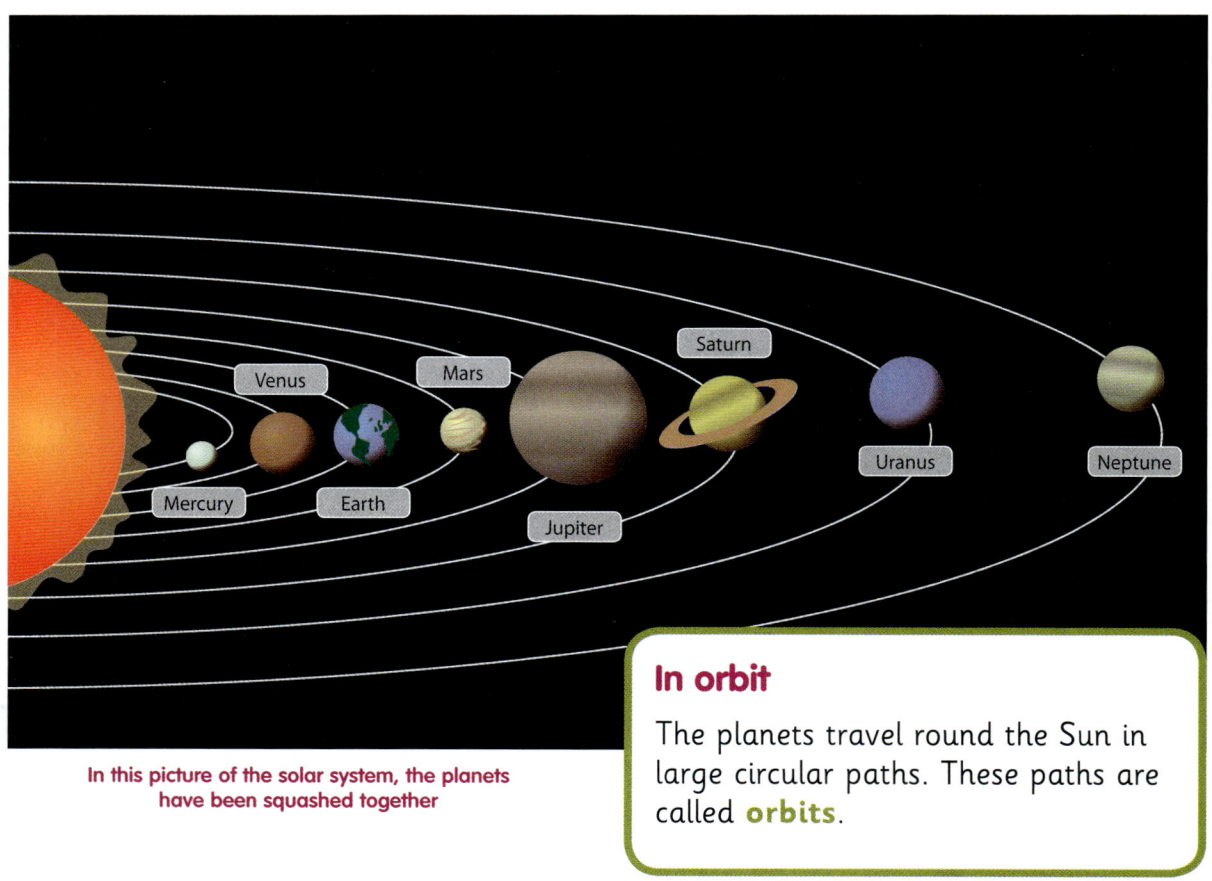

In this picture of the solar system, the planets have been squashed together

In orbit

The planets travel round the Sun in large circular paths. These paths are called **orbits**.

Things to do

Model planets

- Make a model of the solar system in your classroom.
- Draw the Sun and the planets on card. Cut them out and hang them by thread from the ceiling.
- Are the planets all the same shape? Are they the same size?
- How far from the Sun are they?

I wonder…

Some planets are made of rock. But not all! What else can planets be made from?

Dig deeper

Find out:
- the names of the dwarf planets in the solar system.

Did you know?

- Jupiter is the biggest planet in our solar system. All the other planets could fit inside it!

The children hung their model planets from the ceiling. They could not hang them far enough apart!

Spinning around

Things to learn
- The Earth moves around the Sun in an orbit
- The Earth spins as it moves
- Shadows change during the day.

The Sun appears to move from East to West.

What is moving?

The Sun does not move even though it looks as if it does.

We are **spinning** through space just like children on a roundabout. We don't feel it because everything around us is spinning too.

Things to do

Shadow stick

Look at the shadow of a stick in the ground. How does it change from morning to afternoon?

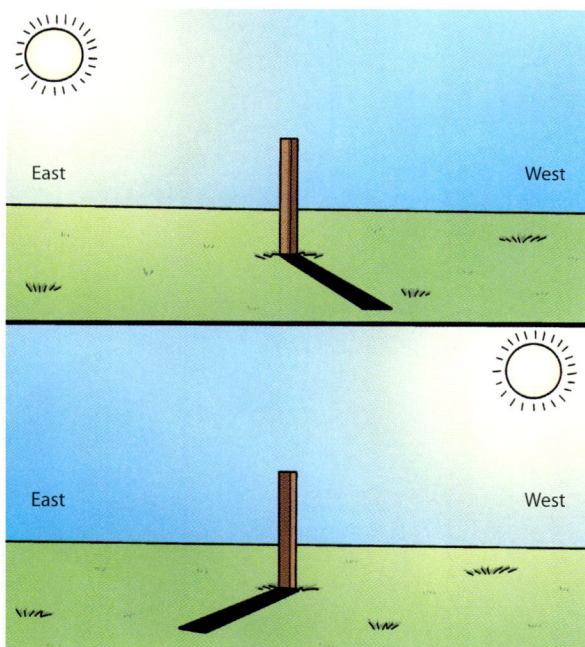

Indoor shadows

Stick a pencil in some clay. Use a torch as your light source.

- Change the position of the torch.
- Who can make the longest shadow?
- How can you make a shadow that is very short?

I wonder…

What happens when the Sun rises and sets?

Dig deeper

Find out:
- about Galileo
- what he found out about the Sun.

Galileo Galilei

Did you know?

- Because the Earth is spinning, you are moving at about 1000 km per hour with the Earth.

Moving shadows

Things to learn
- Shadows change during the day
- We can use changing shadows to tell the time

Dangerous light

Tamara and Leila have been set a difficult and exciting task.

- Can you help them?
- How can they track how the Sun seems to move if they can't look at it?

Never look at the Sun directly. It can damage your eyes.

How can we track how the Sun seems to move without looking at it?

Things to do

Telling the time

The mechanical clocks we have today were not invented until about 700 years ago. Before then people used the Sun to tell the time of day. They used **sundials**.

A sundial - what does it show?

The shadow cast by the **gnomon** (the central stick) onto the dial shows what time it is.

I wonder...
Why don't we use sundials today? Why are clocks better?

Dig deeper
Find out:
- about Ibn al-Haytham and how he divided the day into equal hours.

Did you know?
- The first sundial was made in Ancient Egypt. You had to turn it round at midday

An Egyptian sundial looked like this. The 'T' cast a shadow. You told the time by the shadow length

Unit 5: Earth and beyond

Happy Birthday Earth!

Things to learn
- The Earth, Sun and Moon are all spheres (shaped like a ball)
- The Earth moves around the Sun
- It takes the Earth one year to orbit the Sun.

The Earth is a sphere

Spacemen were the first to see the sphere of the Earth.

People knew the Earth was spherical before we went into space.

As ships sail away from land, the bottom part of the boat disappears before the sails. This would not happen if the Earth was flat.

The first astronauts saw the Earth as a sphere

In a lunar eclipse, the Earth casts a shadow on the Moon. The shadow is round.

What appears first on the horizon?

Things to do

What is a year?

You measure how old you are in years. It is one year between one of your birthdays and the next. If you counted every day between your birthdays you would count 365 days.

A long trip

It takes 365 days or one year for the Earth to travel once around the Sun.

As the Earth orbits the Sun, the seasons change.

Winter

Summer

I wonder...
Do all planets take the same time to orbit the Sun?

Dig deeper
Find out:
- the difference between the seasons in other countries.

Unit 5: Earth and beyond

Night and day

Things to learn
- The Earth spins on its axis
- It takes 24 hours to spin round once
- 24 hours is one day.

Why do we have day and night?

The Earth spins on its **axis**. The axis is an imaginary line which runs from the North Pole at the 'top' of the Earth to the South Pole at the 'bottom'.

Half of the Earth is night and half is day

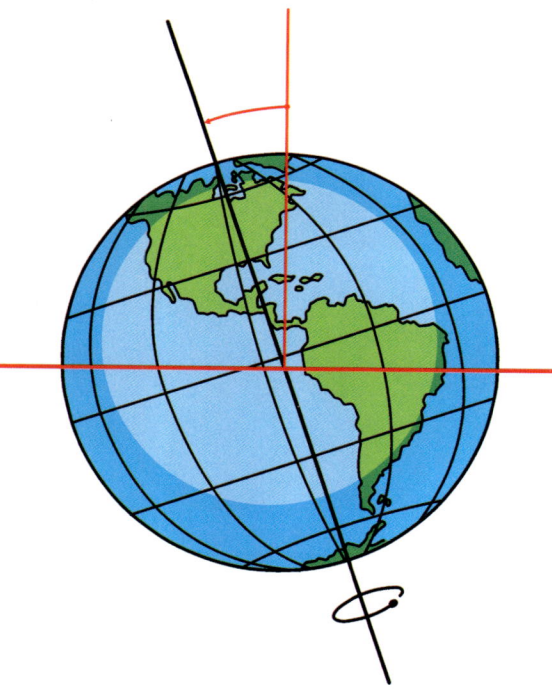

The Earth takes a whole day to turn once

- At any time half the Earth faces the Sun. For this part of the Earth it is day.
- The other half of the Earth faces away from the Sun. It receives no light. For this part of the Earth it is night.

Things to do

Make a day

Use a globe as your Earth. Mark where you live. Your torch is the Sun so it must not move. Make the globe spin so that when half of the world is lit up, the other half is in darkness.

Dig deeper

Find out:
- where on the Earth it is night when it is day where you live.

Did you know?

- Canadian circus owner Guy Laliberte became the first clown in space. In 2009 he visited the International Space Station and he orbited the Earth.

Guy Laliberte

I wonder...

Are days on other planets the same length as on Earth?

Unit 5: Earth and beyond

Unit 5: Review

What have you learned?

- The Earth is a planet.
- The Sun is our nearest star.
- The Earth is one of eight known planets in the solar system.
- The Sun is the star at the centre of the solar system.
- The Earth moves around the Sun in an orbit.
- As the Earth moves, it spins on its axis.
- In the daytime the Sun casts shadows.
- Shadows change during the day.
- The Sun appears to move from East to West.
- We can use changing shadows to tell the time.
- The Earth, Sun and Moon are all spherical (shaped like a ball).
- It takes the Earth one year to orbit the Sun.
- It takes the Earth 24 hours to spin round once on its axis.
- 24 hours is one day.

Find out more about…

- space travel
- who was the first person to see the Earth from space
- whether people may ever live on the Moon.

Check-up

Hassan is making a model of the Earth, Sun and Moon. He is using a beach ball, a tennis ball and a pea.

- Which should he choose for each?
- Draw what his model might look like.

The answer!

Remember the question about Anjuli's phone call?

The Earth spins on its axis. So when it is day for one half of the world it is night for the other half. Anjuli lives on the other side of the Earth from her aunt. She will be in daytime when her aunt is in the night.

Unit 1: Living things in the environment checklist

What do you know?
- Think about these statements
- Which do you know? Which can you do?

- I have learned that plants and animals are living things and that they are all organisms
- I can name some different animals and plants in my local environment
- I have learned that a habitat is a place where plants and animals live naturally
- I understand that not all habitats are the same
- I have learned that different plants and animals live in different habitats
- I can point out similarities and differences between plants and animals
- I can group living things in different ways
- I have learned that humans belong to the animal group
- I understand that humans can damage the environment and we should care for it
- I have learned that different places in the world have different weather

Unit 2: Materials checklist

What do you know?
- Think about these statements
- Which do you know? Which can you do?

- I know that everything is made from materials
- I have learned to describe materials in different ways
- I have learned that some materials are natural and some are man-made
- I have learned that rock is under all the Earth's surface
- I have learned that different rocks have different names
- I can describe different rocks
- I can say what happens to rocks when I scratch them
- I can record my results in a table
- I have learned that we use rocks for a variety of jobs
- I know that materials come from different sources
- I have learned that we change some natural materials so we can use them
- I have learned that we can change the shape of some materials by bending, stretching and twisting
- I have learned that some materials change when they are heated
- I have learned that some materials cannot be changed back
- I have learned that some substances dissolve in water and some do not
- I can keep my investigations fair by only changing one variable at a time
- I can record my results in a table
- I have learned that some changes are reversible
- I have learned that some changes are irreversible

Unit 3: Light and dark checklist

What do you know?
- Think about these statements
- Which do you know? Which can you do?

- I know that we need light to see
- I know that when there is no light it is dark
- I have learned that light comes from a source
- I know that some light sources are brighter than others
- I have learned that shiny objects reflect light
- I have learned that the Sun is a source of light
- I have learned that the Sun is our main source of light in the daytime
- I know that looking at the Sun can hurt our eyes
- I know that we use light to help us when it is dark
- I have learned that some materials block light
- I understand that we get shadows when light is blocked
- I have found out that shadows can be changed
- I have learned to plan an investigation
- I can make careful observations
- I have investigated which material makes the best shadow
- I have learned that light travels in straight lines

Unit 4: Electricity checklist

What do you know?
- Think about these statements
- Which do you know? Which can you do?

- I know that electricity can make things move, light up, heat up and produce sound
- I know that some appliances in our homes use mains electricity and some use electricity from batteries
- I know that mains electricity can be dangerous
- I have learned how to make a simple circuit
- I know the names of some components in a circuit
- I have learned how electricity travels around a simple circuit
- I know that circuits can contain different components
- I have learned that a switch breaks the flow of electricity in a circuit
- I can say why some circuits work and some do not
- I have learned how to draw a circuit using symbols
- I know that electricity can be used to make our lives easier

Unit 5: Earth and beyond checklist

What do you know?
- Think about these statements
- Which do you know? Which can you do?

- I have learned that the Earth is a planet
- I have learned that the Sun is our nearest star
- I have learned that the Earth is one of eight known planets in the solar system
- I have learned that the Sun is the star at the centre of the solar system
- I have learned that the Earth travels around the Sun in an orbit
- I know that as it travels, the Earth spins on its axis
- I know that light travels from the Sun to the Earth
- I know that in the daytime the light from the Sun casts shadows
- I know that shadows change during the day
- I can carefully observe and measure shadows
- I have learned that we can use changing shadows to tell the time
- I have learned that the Earth, Sun and Moon are all spherical (shaped like a ball)
- I understand that it takes the Earth one year to orbit the Sun
- I know it takes the Earth 24 hours to spin round once on its axis
- I know that 24 hours is one day

Glossary

appliance – a piece of electrical equipment used in people's homes, such as a cooker or washing machine
artificial – man-made materials
asteroid – a small object that moves around the Sun
axis – imaginary line from the North Pole to the South Pole
battery – a source of electricity
bend (v) – to change something's normal shape
break (n & v) – (n) a space or gap; (v) to stop something working
bright – shining strongly, or with plenty of light
bulb – the glass of an electric light, where the light shines from
buzzer – an electrical component that makes a sound
candle – a stick of wax with a string through the middle, which you burn to give light
change – to become different
circuit – the complete circle that an electric current travels
comet – an object in space like a bright ball with a long tail that moves around the Sun
compare – to examine things to find out how they are similar or different
component – one of the different parts of a circuit
cool (v & adj) – (v) to become colder; (adj) slightly cold
dark – absence of light
day – the light part of the day when you can see the Sun
dissolve – if a solid dissolves, it mixes with a liquid and becomes part of it
Earth – the planet we live on
electricity – the power carried by wires used to make lights and machines work
environment – the place where plants and animals live
extinct – organism that is no longer in the world
flow (v & n) – (v) to move steadily; (n) steady movement

galaxy – a large group of stars
gnomon – the central stick of a sundial
grow – to get bigger by adding material
habitat – the home of plants and animals
heat (v & n) – (v) to make something warmer; (n) when something is warm or hot
hibernate – if an animal hibernates, it sleeps through the winter
hibernation – to sleep all through winter
irreversible – cannot be changed back
light – the brightness from the Sun or a lamp
liquid – a substance such as water, which flows and forms a flat top
mains electricity – electricity which comes from a wall socket
melt – to change from solid to liquid
migrate (v), migration (n) – to travel from one part of the world to another
Milky Way – our home galaxy
minibeast – very small animal without a backbone
Moon – our natural satellite
night – the dark part of the day when you cannot see the Sun
orbit (v & n) – (v) to travel around an object in space; (n) the curved line that a planet moves in as it travels around another object in space
organism – a living thing
planet – a large round object in space that moves around a star
processed – when we do things to a material to change it, e.g. knit wool
property – quality of a material
reflect – to bounce light off a surface
reversible – can be changed back to its original state
shiny – reflects light well
solid – materials that cannot be easily squashed
source – origin
spin – turn on the spot

star – object in space with its own light
stretch – to get longer when pulled
substance – material
Sun – large bright object in the sky that gives us light – our nearest star
sundial – used to tell the time by the Sun
switch – used to make or break a circuit
torch – flashlight; portable light source
transparent – clear, see-through
twist – to change shape when turned
Universe – all the known and unknown world and galaxies in space
weather – the mixture of sunshine, rain and wind
wire – metal strip used to conduct electricity

Index

air 10
airstrips 32
Ancient Egypt 61
animals 4–9
    electricity 53
    environments 3
    fossils 15
    grouping 6–7
    habitats 4–5
    light 29, 33
    natural materials 18
    solar heat 31
    tiny 7
appliances 42
apprentices 51
artificial light 32
artificial materials 18, 19
asteroids 56
axes 64

basins 21
bathrooms 21
batteries 42, 43, 48–9
beans 23
bending light 38
bent materials 21
bicarbonate of soda 24
boats 32, 62
bottles 37
breakfast cereal 23
brightness 28
broken circuits 50
bulbs 44–5, 47–9
buzzers 49

Cacao beans 23
cars 49
cereal 23
chalk 17
changed materials 18
chocolate 22, 23
circuits 44–5, 50–1
clay 18, 20, 21
clocks 61
clothing 10, 19
clouds 43
cold environments 2
comets 56
components 48
conductors 43
cooled rocks 14

darkness 27–40
day time 64–5
deep oceans 33
desert 9
diamonds 17
dissolved materials 24–5
doorbells 49
drills 49
drought 10
dwarf planets 57

Earth 14–15, 39, 43, 55–66
ecology 9

Edison, Thomas 47
electricity 41–54
    circuits 44–5, 50–1
    electricians 51
    model making 48–9
    saving 47
    sparks 41–2
    static 42
    wires 44, 48–9
environments
    caring for 8–9
    definition 2
    ecology 9
    habitats 4–5, 8–9
    sharing 3
    tropical 1
extinction 8
extreme weather 10

fibres 10, 18, 19
flour 24, 25
flowers 6–7
forecasts 11
forests 9
fossils 15

galaxies 55–66
Galileo Galilei 59
gnomon (sundials) 61
gravy powder 24
growth 2

habitats 4–5, 8–9
hard rock 17
hardness of materials 16–17
headlights 49
heat 18, 31
heating up materials 22–3
hibernation 5
hot environments 1, 2
houses 43, 49
humid environments 1
hurricanes 10

indoor shadows 35, 59
International Space Station 65

jungle environments 3

Laliberte, Guy 65
lava 15
layered rocks 14
light 27–40, 60–1
    animals 29, 33
    artificial 32
    bending 38
    cars 49
    day time 64–5
    electricity 44–5, 47–9, 51–2
    night time 30, 32, 64–5
    plants 34
    reflection 29
    runways 32
    sources 28, 38, 39
    street lights 30

light bulbs 44–5, 47–9
lighthouses 32
lightning 43
liquids 22, 24–5
living things 1–12
lunar eclipses 62

mains electricity 42
man-made materials 10, 19
materials 13–26
    artificial 18, 19
    bending 21
    changing 18
    dissolved 24–5
    hardness 16–17
    heating up 22–3
    natural 18–19
    processed 18
    properties 16–17
    reversible changes 20, 21
    twisted 21
mechanical clocks 61
melted rocks 14
melting 14, 22
metal rods 43
metals 21, 43
meteorologists 11
migration 5
Milky Way 55
minibeasts 7
mixtures 23
model making 48–9, 57
Moon 30, 39, 55, 62
moons 56
motors 48–9
mountain environments 2
movement 52

natural materials 18–19
night time 30, 32, 64–5
Nylon 19

oceans 33
orbits 56, 58, 65
organisms 1–12
Owen, Richard 15

planets 14–15, 39, 43, 55–66
plants 4–7, 9–11
    fossils 15
    light 34
plastic bottles 37
Plasticine 20
polarization 49
power 53
processed materials 18
puppets 35, 36–7

rain 10
rain forests 9
reeds 4
reflection of light 29
reversible material changes 20, 21
rice 24, 25
rivers 10

rocks 14–17, 18, 21
rods 43
runway lights 32

salt 24, 25
sea 2, 6, 14
seashore environments 2
seasons 5, 63
shadows 34–5, 38–9, 59, 60–1, 62
shiny objects 29
ships 32, 62
soapstone 17
soft rock 17
solar eclipse 39
solar system 39, 55–66
solids 23
sound 52
sources of light 28, 38, 39
South Americans 23
Space Station 65
spheres 62
spinning orbits 58
stars 10, 30–1, 39, 55, 58
static electricity 42
stone 15, 16
street lights 30
stretched materials 21
strong winds 10
sugars 24, 25
Sun 10, 30–1, 39, 55, 58, 61
sundials 61
surfing 11
Swan, Joseph 47
switches 49

televisions 49
temperature 18, 22–3
time 61, 62–3
toilets 21
tornadoes 10
tropical environments 1
twisted materials 21

unbroken circuits 50
Universe 55–66

volcanoes 15

water 10, 24–5
weather 2, 10–11, 31
wind
    extreme weather 10
    measuring 11
    power 53
wires 44, 48–9
wood 18
wool 18
worms 4

year definition 63